SUBHAS CHANDRA BOSE

A Life from Beginning to End

Copyright © 2020 by Hourly History.

All rights reserved.

Table of Contents

Introduction
Early Life
Expelled from School
Work in London
Developing His Ideology
By the Führer's Side
Going Over to the Japanese
Bose's Invasion of India
The Fatal Plane Crash
India After Subhas Chandra Bose
Conclusion

Introduction

Subhas Chandra Bose was a revolutionary who sought Indian independence, but as many would contend, he ended up on the wrong side of history. In order to shake off the British yoke, Bose enlisted aid from Germany and Japan during World War II. This has led some to roundly condemn Bose as nothing more than a fascist cast in the same mold as Adolf Hitler, Hideki Tojo, and Benito Mussolini. But is there more to this complicated figure than meets the eye?

In this book, we will take a look at the big picture when it comes to one of India's first freedom fighters of the modern era.

Chapter One

Early Life

"One individual may die for an idea, but that idea will, after his death, incarnate itself in a thousand lives."

—Subhas Chandra Bose

Born on January 23, 1897, Subhas Chandra Bose was the middling child of a well-to-do family eking out an existence in British-controlled India. He was the ninth of fourteen children born to his parents, Janakinath and Prabhabati Bose.

Janakinath was an attorney and a good provider for the family. He was held in high esteem among the 40,000 some residents of Bose's hometown of Cuttack. Cuttack served as an administrative center during the British regime, and more affluent Indian families were made into a semi-autonomous ruling class. It was on the back of Janakinath's earnings that Bose received his education. He attended the best schools in India, beginning his formal education at a European-styled elementary school of the colonial tradition. Bose often found the curriculum distasteful, however, resenting its suppression of Indian culture in favor of European values.

His outlook would change dramatically when, in 1909, he enrolled at India's Ravenshaw Collegiate School. Unlike his elementary school, Ravenshaw taught a combined curriculum of British and Indian studies. The school's staff was also predominantly Indian. Here, Bose would defy his previous British taskmasters and delve into all things Hindu, from poetry and philosophy to yogic exercises. More importantly, young Bose would meet an inspiring mentor in the form of the school's headmaster, Beni Madhab Das, who would leave him with lessons in not just reading, writing, and arithmetic but also in national consciousness.

It was in the auspices of Ravenshaw that much of Bose's revolutionary spirit was awakened, but it would take much more adversity, and even a world war, to bring it to the surface.

Chapter Two
Expelled from School

"Nationalism is inspired by the highest ideals of the human race, stayam [the true], shivam [the god], Sundaram [the beautiful]. Nationalism in India has roused the creative faculties which for centuries had been lying dormant in our people."

—Subhas Chandra Bose

Bose managed to keep his grades up at Ravenshaw, and at the age of 16, he entered Calcutta's Presidency College. Here, he was greatly influenced by the writings of the Indian guru Swami Vivekananda. Vivekananda had passed away in 1902 at just 39 years of age, but he had preached a message that seemed to capture the mood of the populace at the time. His declaration for Indians to reach for their "own salvation" while finding a better means to "service humanity" became many a young man's rallying call, and Bose was one of them. Bose would take this universal call for the betterment of the human individual and transform it into a nationalistic call for the betterment of the Indian people as a whole. For Bose, there would soon be nothing better than living for the service of the nation.

Bose envisioned a whole nation of Indians coming together for the greater good. He would later take as his mantra, "The naked Indian, the illiterate Indian, the

Brahman Indian, the pariah Indian is my brother!" Such thinking, of course, was quite contrary to the caste system that had been so entrenched in Indian society, in which the higher classes segregated and ostracised the lowest class, the so-called untouchables, out of hand. As merely a teenager, Subhas Chandra Bose was creating a new worldview for Indian society that wished to bring all elements of the subcontinent together once and for all.

Just as Bose was dreaming of national unity, however, the rest of the world seemed poised to fall apart. It was right around this time in 1914 that the world stumbled into the great war that would become known as World War I. It was India's colonial overlords, the British, that seemed to have the most to lose in this conflict. Many wondered if the British Empire might indeed break apart completely. Hopeful Indians, such as Bose, could only wonder if this might be the case.

Bose's time in the college would be interrupted when on January 10, 1916, while he was immersed in his books in the library, a fellow student informed him that a British instructor at the school, Edward Farley Oaten, had maltreated some of the students. Bose was a class representative, so he took it upon himself to see whether or not the rumor was true. Upon hearing of the allegation, he went to the school principal, Henry R. James, to see if he could get Oaten censured for his actions.

But according to the professor's side of the story, he had merely sought to curtail a group of rowdy students making noise outside of the classroom by taking them by the arm to escort them elsewhere. In Oaten's view, he had done nothing wrong, and therefore there was no need to apologize. The principal did not have the authority to force the man to apologize either. This enraged Bose and prompted him to organize a strike the very next day. Word of the strike spread like wildfire around the town, and several nearby schools erupted in strikes and protests as well.

In the midst of all this drama, Oaten finally met with the pupils he had offended and managed to broker a cessation of the protests. The principal, meanwhile, decided to fine the students five rupees each. Even worse, despite his previous contrition, Oaten then ordered several of those who were involved in the protest out of his class and shortly afterward manhandled yet another student. This infuriated Bose and his peers and inspired them to take matters into their own hands.

So it was in mid-February that several students caught Oaten off-guard at the bottom of Presidency College's main staircase and pummeled him with their fists. The whole ordeal transpired in less than a minute, but as the perpetrators scattered, Bose was among those seen fleeing from the waylaid professor. This resulted in Bose's suspension and ultimate expulsion from the school. Bose would never admit responsibility in the incident, but neither did he deny it later in life. Right or wrong, it was over the crumpled body of one beaten Professor Oaten that Subhas Chandra Bose's seeds of revolution had been sown.

Chapter Three

Work in London

"Life loses half its interest if there is no struggle—if there are no risks to be taken. . . . It is not possible to serve one's country in the best and fullest manner if one is chained to the Civil Service. In short, national and spiritual aspirations are not compatible with obedience to Civil Service Examinations."

—Subhas Chandra Bose

In the aftermath of his expulsion, Bose attempted to appeal the decision, claiming to have been a witness rather than a participant. The principal wasn't convinced, however, and roundly condemned Bose as an agitator and refused to entertain any appeals he attempted to lodge with the institution. His parents meanwhile were horrified, with his mother in particular refusing to believe that her son would resort to violence against school faculty.

Bose losing his position at school sent his father scrambling to find another place of higher learning that would accept the young man. With no small effort, after asking around, Janakinath finally found it at the University of Calcutta's Scottish Church College. The school still exists to this day and stands as the longest-running Christian liberal arts school on the Indian subcontinent.

Even Bose's idol, Swami Vivekananda, was at one time in attendance at this very same school.

Despite the previous turmoil he had been involved in, Bose managed to graduate from the university with a bachelor's degree in philosophy in 1918. This then served as a springboard for Bose to go to England in the fall of 1919 under the pretense of studying for the Indian Civil Services exam. In British India, working for the Indian Civil Services was in many ways the highest-level post that native Indians could hope to attain. It was the fast track to becoming a high paid bureaucrat in the British Raj, ruling over the lower-class masses. Bose himself never thought that he was going to pass his examinations and was mostly trying to appease his father.

In fact, when Bose mentioned what he was doing to one of his professors at Presidency College, a man who was himself a Cambridge Alumni, the man openly scoffed that Bose was wasting his time and "throwing away tens of thousands of rupees" by paying the entrance fee. This didn't matter too much to Bose, however, since it wasn't his idea in the first place. As such, in the face of this slight, he simply shrugged and remarked, "My father wants me to throw away the ten thousand rupees."

Washing his hands of what the outcome might be, at the wishes of his father, Bose left for Britain on board the SS *City of Calcutta* on September 15, 1919. After a weeklong stopover in the Suez Canal, he arrived in England on October 25. He was quite late, and due to the delay of his arrival, Bose had to rush to consult with an academic advisor in order to gain late enrolment to his classes. He was eventually directed to head to Cambridge University, where he met up with a certain Mr. Reddaway, the director of Fitzwilliam Hall, who encouraged him to sign on for a philosophy degree.

In pursuit of this, Bose enrolled at Cambridge's Fitzwilliam College on November 19. His main coursework included classes in Sanskrit, English, European history, political science, English law, economics, geography, and of course, philosophy. Of these classes, he was most intrigued by history and political science, the latter of which he would engage in lengthy debates with his peers. He also felt that such coursework helped him to get a feel for "the inner currents of international politics."

Although such coursework was merely a means to an end—with that end being his examinations for the civil service—Bose relished the former and dreaded the latter. Nevertheless, fulfilling his father's wishes, he began testing for the civil service in the summer of 1920. The testing lasted several weeks, and Bose was sure he had failed, but to his disbelief, he not only passed but managed to snag the fourth-highest score. This should have been good news, but Bose knew that it meant he would be forced to work for the British government and, not wishing to be a lackey of the British, he began to distance himself from the very thing he had fought so hard to achieve.

During this time, Bose began to write home about his misgivings. In particular, he wrote to his older brother Sarat. In one of his letters, Bose declared that his decision to resign from the civil service in favor of his revolutionary ideals "is final and unchangeable." He believed that only by struggling on Indian soil for Indians could independence on a national level be achieved. No matter what, Bose wanted to be of aid in India's struggle for independence, and he viewed the civil service as being completely contrary to that goal.

Janakinath was far from happy with his son's attitude. It was in order to persuade the old man to change his mind that Bose fired off a letter directly to him on April 6, 1921. In his strong-willed defiance to submit to the British Raj, Bose even referenced the biblical story of Jacob when he asked his father, "Should we under the present circumstances own allegiance to a foreign bureaucracy and sell ourselves for a mess of pottage?"

Bose believed that remaining in the lucrative post for the civil service would have given him the trappings of wealth and prestige, but only at the cost of selling the free and independent India he so longed to bring about. Janakinath meanwhile insisted that his son just needed to be patient since recent reforms indicated that India would be on the path to home rule sooner or later. Bose wanted it sooner rather than later, however, and was more than willing to precipitate it by force, or as he wrote to his brother at the time, "Only on the soil of sacrifice and suffering can we raise our national edifice." It is quite remarkable that such radical dialogue could be sent back and forth between Britain and India without any of the British minders picking it up, but this appears to have been the case.

While Bose debated with his father whether to wait for reform or become a revolutionary, a lawyer and activist by the name of Mahatma Gandhi was engineering a much gentler revolution of his own, focusing on resistance through completely non-violent means. Bose would inherently view such efforts as weakness, but he nevertheless respected Gandhi's efforts as a leader in the independence movement.

Back in Britain meanwhile, Bose abruptly resigned from the Indian Civil Service on April 23, 1921. Despite anything his father might say, he believed that a decided detour in his destiny was needed. Bose was determined to chart his own unique path toward Indian revolution and independence. As confirmation, he fired off another letter to his brother back home, writing, "The die is cast, and I earnestly hope that nothing but good will come out of it."

Chapter Four

Developing His Ideology

"I have no doubt in my mind that our chief national problems relating to the eradication of poverty, illiteracy and disease and the scientific production and distribution can be tackled only along socialistic lines."

—Subhas Chandra Bose

Immediately after Bose's sudden resignation, several of his professors and other members of faculty at Cambridge attempted to persuade him to reconsider. Bose, now 24 years old, was resolute and refused to budge from his decision. Shortly thereafter, he got on a ship and headed back to India, arriving at a port in Bombay on June 16, 1921.

The first person he went to see was the resident dissident, Mahatma Gandhi, that he had heard so much about while he was away in England. He found the spiritual leader seated in a room on top of Indian-styled carpeting. Around him were disciples on all sides, all wearing khadi, traditional Indian hand-spun clothing. Seeing them dressed in this manner made Bose feel a little bit guilty about his business casual attire, prompting him to apologize for his outfit. The easy-going Gandhi took no offense and simply smiled at the young man and sought to make him more comfortable.

Taking a seat in front of the guru, Bose then began to question Gandhi about his efforts and in particular asked him how his non-violent approach would help broker independence for India. After a lengthy discussion, Bose was given a post for the Indian National Congress, the political party for which Gandhi served as president. Despite differences the two men may have had, at Gandhi's direction, Bose was sent to Calcutta to be under the employ of fellow Indian resistance activist, Chittaranjan Das. Das—an advocate of a much more aggressive form of nationalism than Gandhi espoused—would become Bose's mentor during this period. Under his guidance, Bose developed his still nascent ideology for Indian independence.

It was shortly after this that Bose set in motion a general strike and boycott of festivities that were being organized for an upcoming visit by the prince of Wales. The prince was set to land in Bombay on November 17, but Bose and his colleagues were determined to make sure that he received a cold welcome. Bose would later state that it was nothing personal against the prince himself but merely a means of protesting the colonial government in general.

On the heels of this massive protest, Bose began jockeying to become the president of the All India Youth Congress. He was duly elected to this role in 1923. More opportunity then opened up for Bose the following year when his mentor, Chittaranjan Das, was elected the mayor of Calcutta. Das awarded his protegé by giving Bose a posting as the CEO of Calcutta Municipal Corporation. Bose would then continue to lobby for independence until he was arrested in a massive sweep conducted by British colonials in 1925. Because of his links to revolutionary activities, he was sent to a prison in Mandalay.

Bose's time in prison was fraught with hardship, and he suffered a bad bout of tuberculosis during the term he was given. After a couple of years served, he was released in 1927. If the prevailing authorities felt that prison time would slow Bose down, however, they were gravely mistaken. It was that same year that he was made general secretary of the Indian National Congress. Acting in this capacity, Bose began to work closely with Jawaharlal Nehru, a notable freedom activist and future prime minister of India.

Before long, Bose established the GOC Congress Volunteer Corps, a makeshift volunteer militia of uniformed freedom fighters. Shortly after that, he was again arrested for civil disobedience. While in prison, he was elected mayor of Calcutta, a post he would hold until April 15, 1931. After he was released from prison and subsequently rearrested several more times, Bose was exiled from India by the British. His fight against British rule would have to continue from outside the country.

Chapter Five

By the Führer's Side

"I am convinced that if we do desire freedom we must be prepared to wade through blood."

—Subhas Chandra Bose

After leaving his post as mayor of Calcutta, for much of the rest of the 1930s, Subhas Chandra Bose went on a world tour in which he would visit several key locations around the world. It was at this time that he first developed an interest in fascism, and as such, he paid a visit to its source: the stomping grounds of Italy's Benito Mussolini.

Here, Bose bore witness to how fascist groups were organized and how authoritarianism might be used to break apart the hegemony of Britain and bring about the freedom of India. Such notions would later form the basis of Bose's book *The Indian Struggle*, which shined a spotlight on the revolutionary actions of India from 1920 to 1934. Ironically enough, even though the book championed shaking off the British yoke, it was through the use of British printing presses that it was published. First printed by a publisher in London in 1935, *The Indian Struggle* wasn't allowed to circulate for very long before British authorities realized how dangerous the book's sentiments might be to the status quo. Soon after its first publication, the book was outright banned.

Around this time, Bose became intimately involved with a woman by the name of Emilie Schenkl, who had served as his secretary. Bose allegedly married Ms. Schenkel in 1937 during a secret wedding ceremony, although no records of the marriage remain. The pair went onto have one child together, a girl named Anita. The whole relationship has long been shrouded in secrecy—so much so that Bose's own brother Sarat did not learn anything about it until 1947, two years after Bose's death. Even then, it was rumored that Emilie was merely a fling with whom Bose had a love child. At any rate, Bose apparently felt he had matters more important than marriage to deal with because upon his eventual return to India, he didn't even mention it.

India in the late 1930s was once again a hotbed of dissent. As anti-British sentiment heated up, Bose was arrested in the spring of 1936 before he was set free once again in March of 1937. Regardless of the crackdown on the writings of Bose, they could not suppress his ideology entirely, and soon he was able to stir the consciousness of India to such an extent that in 1938 he was nominated as the president of the Indian National Congress.

It was here that he first made a loud call to arms against the British government, a move that brought him in direct opposition to the other Indian independence leader, Mahatma Gandhi. As such, Gandhi became a staunch critic and opponent of the Bose administration, creating an irreparable schism within the Indian National Congress party. Bose tried to circumvent the stressors that led to a break, but it proved irreversible. As the divide grew, he also lost support from Nehru, who had previously been a friendly associate.

Still, Bose's popularity soared, and the following year, he was duly re-elected. He achieved this despite Gandhi's dogged stumping for an opposition candidate named Pattabhi Sitaramayya, who was more to his liking. Even though Bose was successfully re-elected, Gandhi and his faction managed to work up enough havoc among the Congress Working Committee members that Bose was ultimately ousted and forced to tender his resignation. After leaving his posting at the Indian National Congress in 1939, Bose was determined to create his own party, which he did by establishing the All India Forward Bloc, which then became a significant faction of the Indian National Congress.

Support for the All India Forward Bloc was primarily located in Bose's home state of Bengal, but to the alarm of British colonials and Gandhi loyalists, it was quickly gaining steam in surrounding regions as well. Bose gained a solid ally in the form of activist Muthuramalinga Thevar, who was an avid disciple of Bose's ideology from the start. It was Thevar that arranged for Bose to pay a visit to Madurai on September 6, 1939, and put together a massive rally to greet his arrival. On the way there, Bose passed through Madras and even spent a few days on Gandhi's Peak.

Meanwhile, he corresponded with several British Labour Party leaders, hoping to enlist support from liberal British representatives. These efforts would not produce any results, and shortly thereafter, Britain would be embroiled in the outbreak of World War II.

Upon Britain's declaration of war in early September, Bose was incensed to find that the British Viceroy of India, Lord Linlithgow, had decided to proclaim India's allegiance to Britain and solidarity against Germany without even consulting the Indian National Congress to broker the terms for such an announcement. It was in outrage of these developments that Bose set off massive protests and demonstrations on the streets of Calcutta and the surrounding region.

In the course of these demonstrations, Bose also led a call to have the Holwell Monument, which many Indians despised, demolished. The monument stood as a dark reminder of the so-called "Black Hole of Calcutta," an infamous dungeon dating back to the 1700s. The dungeon was actually a small holding cell in a fort that belonged to the East India Company. This was prior to official British control of India, and the East India Company was a commercial organization with quasi-colonial claims on the region. The native powerhouse in India at the time was the Mughal Empire. It was the native son of this power block, Siraj al-Dawlah, that had his armies overrun the East India Company's Fort William in Calcutta and afterward crammed 146 prisoners into the holding cell.

The next morning, the dungeon was opened, and John Zephaniah Holwell, a British physician that had been among those imprisoned inside, recorded the horrid details for posterity. Holwell claimed that only 23 of the original 146 prisoners were still alive, and many of them just barely. It was his report of this incident that kicked off a whirlwind propaganda campaign in Britain to take on the Mughal Empire and seize official control of India once and for all.

As such, rather than remember or memorialize such a site, most Indians wanted the monument removed. It is for this and other reasons that the grounds of the Holwell Monument became a flashpoint of protests. As a result of his participation in these demonstrations, Bose was yet again arrested and put in chains by the British. Bose was determined not to let this stop him, and after he staged a weeklong hunger strike, the beleaguered British set him free. Even so, Bose was placed under strict scrutiny, watched by the British secret police at all times.

Apparently, this wasn't quite enough, because Bose soon managed to slip away from his British handlers. Starting in early 1941, he managed to travel all the way to Afghanistan, through the Soviet Union, and on to Germany. It was here that Bose hoped he could somehow foster a deal with none other than the Nazi Führer, Adolf Hitler, which he hoped would help bolster the Indian resistance movement against their common enemy, Great Britain.

About three days before his great escape, Bose pretended to be in the midst of spiritual meditation; he had grown a beard and spent his days in fasting and contemplation. Then, late into the night of January 16, 1941, he threw on a long, brown coat over his monkish pajamas and took to the street. Thanks to this subterfuge, he managed to slip through his British minders' grasp, reaching a train station in Bihar, India on January 17. From there, he secured passage to Peshawar.

By the time his British watchers were alerted to his disappearance, Bose was dining with an associate of his named Akbar Shah. He was then offered a stay in the house of a certain Abad Khan before venturing north to

Afghanistan. Here, he was gifted with an Italian passport from the Italian embassy in Kabul before crossing the border into the Soviet Union. In the Soviet Union, Bose traveled with the Italian passport he brandished and, claiming to be an Italian national by the name of Count Orlando Mazzota, secured passage to Rome. It was from Rome, the old capital of the Roman Empire, that Bose would venture on to the capital of Hitler's Third Reich: Berlin, Germany.

In Germany, he received a warm welcome from Hitler's foreign minister, Joachim von Ribbentrop. Yet as friendly as von Ribbentrop might have been, he found the response from other German officials lukewarm at best. Several initial appointments with high figures in the Nazi government were delayed or denied, but eventually he did manage to enlist the aid of Germany's Special Bureau for India and was given access to German-Indian propaganda by way of the radio station Azad Hind Radio.

Of much more consequence was the fact that Bose was able to form an entire Indian Legion made up of some 4,500 Indian troops. Interestingly enough, these troops were captured prisoners of the Germans, apprehended in wars with Britain in North Africa. These Indian soldiers had been fighting for the British when they were ensnared by the Germans, but now they agreed to switch sides in order to form a freedom fighting force under Subhas Chandra Bose.

This group of Indian soldiers was initially tied to the German Wehrmacht, before eventually being overseen directly by the Waffen SS. These Indian freedom fighters even had a rallying call that included the words, "I swear by God this holy oath that I will obey the leader of the German race and state, Adolf Hitler, as the commander of the German armed forces in the fight for India, whose leader is Subhas Chandra Bose!"

Bose also started introducing himself with a new title. He was to be known as *Netaji*, a word which translates as "respected leader" in English. Even more startling, Netaji translates as "Führer" in German—a fact certainly not missed by Bose's Nazi benefactors.

Chapter Six

Going Over to the Japanese

"It is blood alone that can pay the price of freedom. Give me blood and I will give you freedom!"

—Subhas Chandra Bose

Initially, Subhas Chandra Bose was entirely enthusiastic about his newfound support in Nazi Germany, but cracks in his relationship with the Germans began to show early on. The first issue of concern for Bose was when in the summer of 1941, Hitler made the decision to invade the Soviet Union. Bose, an admirer of Soviet Russia, was deeply disturbed to have his German benefactors waging war against the Soviet regime, which he saw as an ally in the fight against the British.

As his anxiety grew, Bose managed to secure a meeting with Hitler himself in 1942. This meeting did little to make Bose feel better, and he left it with the distinct impression that Hitler was much more talk than action when it came to the independence of India. Hitler did not appear to prioritize Indian independence at all but rather seemed to exploit the situation for the sake of propaganda.

As his discontent with Germany grew, Bose began to look toward the other big player of the Axis, Imperial Japan, for support. Japan, after all, was already hammering away at British possessions in Southeast Asia. Believing that this fellow Asian nation just might offer more real-world help in India's struggle, Bose hopped on a German U-boat in 1943 and charged headlong under the war-torn waters of the Atlantic all the way to the southern tip of Africa.

The vessel that carried him then made a sharp left turn and dropped the burgeoning Indian militant nationalist off on the island of Madagascar. It was here that Bose connected with Japanese agents and was ushered onto a Japanese sub to make his way to the Japanese Home Islands. When he arrived in Japan proper, it was first indicated that Bose might lead a pro-Japanese group of Indian fighters. This group was partially an idea of the Japanese Major Iwaichi Fujiwara. Fujiwara's express mission was to create "an army which would fight alongside the Japanese army."

The Japanese at this point were shaking the British out of many of their colonies, thereby making the Japanese a natural ally in the mind of Bose since they shared a common enemy in the Brits. In early 1942, the Japanese under the guidance of General Yamashita had managed to sneak in through British Singapore's backdoor and completely overrun the territory. It was from this staging ground that the so-called India National Army, or as it is otherwise known, the INA, would be established.

By late 1942, however, due to seemingly intractable differences with key Indian players on the ground, plans for this early phase of the INA would be abruptly aborted. It wasn't until the emergence of Subhas Chandra Bose on Singapore's shores in the summer of 1943 that these previously scrapped plans would be reinstated.

The Japanese had learned through their contacts that Bose was a highly respected leader of the Indian resistance movement and, as such, they had high expectations that he would be able to salvage the wreckage of what had been the first incarnation of the INA. Shortly after landing in Singapore, Bose attended a high stakes meeting in this regard, during which the leadership of the INA was officially placed into Bose's hands. Under the stewardship of Bose, Indian nationals living in Southeast Asia were steered into the ranks of the Indian National Army.

On July 5, 1943, Bose declared to the INA volunteers, "Today is the proudest day of my life. Today it has pleased Providence to give me the unique privilege and honour of announcing to the whole world that India's Army of Liberation has come into being. This Army has now been drawn up in military formation on the battle field of Singapore which was once the bulwark of the British Empire. This is not only the Army that will emancipate India from the British yoke, it is also the Army that will hereafter create the future National Army of Free India! Comrades! Let your battle cry be—To Delhi! To Delhi!"

Inspired by Bose's passionate call to arms, several did indeed rally to his promise of storming Delhi and liberating the Indian subcontinent once and for all. And it wasn't only Indian men that rallied to the INA's banner—women also arrived in droves to see what they could do for the cause of independence. In light of this enthusiasm, Bose created a special women's unit that he called the Rani of Jhansi Regiment, led by a female captain named Lakshmi Swaminathan. This made the Indian National Army among the very few armed groups of World War II to include women in their infantry.

The day after Bose made his famous proclamation, he personally oversaw a victory parade of the INA with none other than Japan's prime minister, Hideki Tojo, in attendance. The day of Bose's official coronation as supreme commander of the Indian National Army then came on August 26, 1943.

The next major milestone came on October 21 when Bose established the Provisional Government of Free India, naming himself head of state, prime minister, minister of war, and minister of foreign affairs. Seizing the solemnity of the moment, Bose proclaimed, "In the name of God I take this sacred oath that to liberate India and 38 crores of my countrymen, I Subhas Chandra Bose, will continue the sacred war of freedom till the last breath of my life. . . . Even after winning freedom I will always be prepared to shed the last drop of my blood for the preservation of Indian Freedom."

After these arrangements were made, in November of 1943, Bose made a trip to Japan, where he was in attendance for the Greater East Asia Conference. Japan's so-called Greater East Asia Co-Prosperity Sphere was a propagandized claim that Japan was working to help bolster free and independent partners in Asia that could work together with Japan to create a sphere in which all could prosper. As good as all of this might have sounded, however, most of the time this was far from the truth. All one would have to do is ask someone in Korea or occupied parts of China where the native populations were routinely brutalized by Japanese soldiers, and they would quickly learn that co-prosperity was not always the number one objective of Japanese policy in Asia.

Nevertheless, the Japanese did make good on two immediate promises for Bose and his Provisional Government of Free India; it was decided that Bose's Free India would have control over the Andaman and Nicobar Islands, which had been recently seized from the British. Thousands of Indians loyal to Britain died in the defense of these territories, and perhaps fittingly enough, Bose renamed the Andamans where so much Indian blood had already been spilled *Shahid Dweep*, which translates to "Martyr Island."

Next, Bose planned to launch an assault on British India proper.

Chapter Seven

Bose's Invasion of India

"As soldiers, you will always have to cherish and live up to the three ideals of faithfulness, duty and sacrifice. Soldiers who always remain faithful to their nation, who are always prepared to sacrifice their lives are invincible. If you, too, want to be invincible, engrave these three ideals in the innermost core of your hearts."

—Subhas Chandra Bose

Bose and the INA's invasion into mainland India would become known as the Imphal campaign due to it being centered around the Indian border town of Imphal. Imphal was the capital city of India's Manipur state, nestled in a sweeping plateau in India's northeastern borderlands. The campaign formed part of the Japanese Operation U-Go, an offensive which aimed to capture India, thereby cutting off the supply routes to the Allied front in northern Burma.

Although Bose was the commander of the INA, he was directed by General Renya Mutaguchi, who controlled Japanese troops in Burma. Mutaguchi figured that having the Indian army attack Imphal would serve a secondary purpose of diverting and delaying British forces poised to attack Japanese positions in Burma.

Although the INA would partially serve as a diversion, it was indeed Bose's first opportunity to take the fight right to the British in India. He took it very seriously. It is said that in the days leading up to the attack, Bose would closely inspect and review his troops, making sure that they had everything they needed and were in the best shape possible for the impending invasion.

After several weeks of intensive drilling, the Imphal campaign would begin in earnest on March 15, 1944. Traveling through Burma and over the Indian border, initially the battle—or complete lack thereof—seemed to go well for the Indian-Japanese fighting force. The INA and their Japanese allies charged right through the mountains just in time to completely upend the shocked British troops on the other side. In a matter of days, Imphal was completely surrounded, with Bose hailing the result as being the "glorious and brilliant actions of the brave forces of the Azad Hind Fauj." This was followed by the seizure of the nearby Indian town of Kohima on April 6.

Bose was ecstatic, and after reaching out to Japanese Prime Minister Tojo, he had the Japanese confirm that all conquered territory would be explicitly placed under the rule of his Provisional Government of Free India. Planning for what he hoped would be a string of victories, Bose then selected Indian Major-General Chatterjee as the governor of the newly gleaned territory.

Bose also made sure to officially link the legion he had formed in Nazi Germany with the INA troops in India. In his excitement, he declared it to be a glorious day for the resistance, but he appears to have spoken a little too soon. Shortly thereafter, the British were able to launch a counterattack against the INA troops that were besieging Imphal. The encircled British troops had been kept alive by daring airlifts, during which Allied planes had dropped supplies on top of the defenders. Now, reinforcements had arrived on the ground to link up with the survivors and push the Indian-Japanese forces back. The Axis aggressors were forced to go on the defensive and, having to flee back through treacherous jungle, ended up being killed by pestilent diseases such as malaria, cholera, or dysentery, just as much as they were mowed down by British bullets.

On July 8, Imperial Japan considered the battle completely lost and ordered those who survived to retreat. It is rather interesting that for Japan, who prided itself on never giving ground and often fighting to the last man, the Imphal campaign was one of the few times that the Japanese high command ordered a tactical retreat.

Bose himself was rather dumbfounded by the order for withdrawal. To one of his associates, an Indian named Kawabe, he declared at the time, "Though the Japanese Army has given up the operation, we will continue it. We will not repent even if the advance of our revolutionary army to attain independence of our homeland is completely defeated. Increase in casualties, cessation in supplies, and famine are not reasons enough to stop marching. Even if the whole army becomes only spirit, we will not stop advancing toward our homeland. This is the spirit of our revolutionary army."

Of course, all of these things were easy enough for Bose to say from the comfort of his command headquarters—not so much for those that were on the ground suffering through horrid conditions and diseases. After their harried withdrawal, of the joint Indian-Japanese invasion force that had swept over the Indian border, only about half would survive the trek back. This was the sad reality that Bose's great and glorious dream had woken up to.

Chapter Eight

The Fatal Plane Crash

"It is our duty to pay for our liberty with our own blood. The freedom that we shall win through our sacrifice and exertions, we shall be able to preserve with our own strength."

—Subhas Chandra Bose

By mid-1944, the Axis Powers that Subhas Chandra Bose had placed so much stock in were in a perilous state. Mussolini's fascism was on life support in Northern Italy. German forces were being pushed back by the Russians. And towards the end of the year, Japanese troops had pulled back to Burma's Irrawaddy River, forced to take higher ground against a resurgent British army. As Bose's INA rallied with the Japanese, they would attempt to dig in their heels and make their last stand in Burma.

So it was in the spring of 1945 that the INA took on British incursions in the area of Mandalay in Burma. Soon enough, however, when British troops managed to make their way across the Irrawaddy River, the Indian-Japanese lines all but collapsed. During this desperate hour, it is said that Bose himself showed up to bolster the fighting spirit of his troops, but even his presence wasn't enough to keep the beleaguered INA soldiers fighting. Soon, the British were pushing the Indian-Japanese army right out of Burma.

Japan, meanwhile, had ousted Tojo for his perceived failures and elected a new prime minister.

By April, things were so precarious in Bose's base at Rangoon that he and his associates had to evacuate to Bangkok, Thailand. Shortly thereafter, in May, Rangoon was seized by the British. Bose arrived in Bangkok just in time to receive word that Germany had officially surrendered to the Allies. Now the only main member of the Axis still standing was Japan—and just barely.

Then, on August 15, 1945, after having two atomic bombs dropped on the Home Islands and the Soviet Union making a last-minute declaration of war, Japan finally surrendered. Nevertheless, Bose extolled his troops of the INA to keep fighting. Although the cause certainly seemed hopeless, Bose wasn't willing to give up. On the same day that Japan announced its defeat, Bose issued the following statement to his followers, "In our struggle for the independence of our motherland we have been overwhelmed by an undreamt-of crisis. You may perhaps feel that you have failed in your mission to liberate India. But, let me tell you that this failure is only a temporary nature. No set back and no defeat can undo your positive achievement of the past."

Bose implored them, "Many of you have participated in the fight along the Indo-Burma frontier and also inside India and have gone through hardship and suffering of every sort. Many of your comrades have laid down their lives on that battlefield and have become the immortal heroes of Azad Hind. This glorious sacrifice can never go in vain. Comrades, in this dark hour I call upon you to conduct yourselves with discipline, dignity and strength befitting a truly Revolutionary Army."

Bose and his small band were now pitted against the entirety of the Allied Powers. The only thing that kept them from being squashed outright was their utter obscurity. Italy, Germany, and then Japan had all decisively fallen to the Allied Powers yet Subhas referred to this current set of circumstances as merely a "temporary defeat."

As unlikely as it may seem, Bose then concocted a scheme in which he would seek asylum in Russia. He had always been an admirer of Stalin's Soviet regime and hoped that he could somehow convince the Russian dictator to provide him cover. This great meeting between Bose and Stalin was, however, never meant to be. Shortly after taking off from Bangkok, Bose switched planes in Saigon in order to fly to Dairen, where Bose hoped to link up with Russian officials. The plane then made a stop in modern-day Taipei around noon on August 18 to refuel before continuing on to Dairen.

The plane didn't get very far, however, and shortly after taking off the runway, disaster struck. As it turns out, the plane was overloaded with Japanese evacuees and luggage, and as such, the engine was put under considerable strain just to take to the air. Exceeding its capacity, the plane's portside engine blew up, and the craft plummeted to the ground after lifting just a little over 100 feet in the air. Smashing down nose first, the plane exploded into an inferno of fire.

Incredibly enough, there were survivors, and Bose was one of them. After the crash, he found himself to be relatively unharmed but drenched in gasoline. He and a fellow associate, Habibur Rahman, found their way to the plane's rear exit door, but access was cut off by debris and luggage. It was then that Bose made the fatal mistake of deciding to run through the flames that had erupted immediately in front of them in order to get off the plane through the front exit. As he did so, Bose's gas-drenched clothing ignited. With his arms waving wildly in the air, he ran out of the fiery wreckage, and the rescue team that had assembled outside saw what they could only describe as a "human torch" running toward them.

Efforts were immediately made to put out the flames, but even with this quick-thinking action, the burns Bose sustained were just too dire. Most who saw him assumed that his injuries were fatal, but efforts were made to save him all the same. Bose was immediately rushed to a nearby military hospital where a Japanese doctor named Taneyoshi Yoshimi began emergency treatment of his injuries. It appeared that Bose had suffered massive third-degree burns over most of his body. To treat his charred flesh, the doctor had a disinfecting agent rubbed over his skin before wrapping up his burns in gauze and bandages. During the course of his treatment, Bose was also given a blood transfusion in the hopes of stabilizing his condition. But it was all for naught.

The damage was too extensive, and in a matter of hours, Subhas Chandra Bose would be dead. Despite the pain from the terrible burns, Bose is said to have voiced his desire for India's independence until the very end. Just before passing away, he is said to have declared, "I have fought for India's freedom till the last. Tell my countrymen India will be free before long. Long live free India."

Chapter Nine

India After Subhas Chandra Bose

"Never lose your faith in the destiny of India. There is no power on Earth which can keep India in bondage. India will be free and, that too, soon."

—Subhas Chandra Bose

Subhas Chandra Bose passed away on August 18, 1945, at just 48 years of age. Many believe that if he had been allowed to live, he might have been able to take on a more active role in India's eventual independence.

Immediately after his death, there was great grieving among his followers in the INA, and a general sense of loss among many Indians that knew of Bose's story. In the aftermath of his passing, even Mahatma Gandhi had a few good words to say about him. Gandhi summed up the situation by saying, "Subhas Bose has died well. He was undoubtedly a patriot, though misguided."

As for the INA members that Subhas left behind, the intention of the British was initially to punish them as traitors. It was in this vein that the INA trials were commenced. This inquest was launched in order to figure out how culpable Indian officers were in their collaboration with the Japanese. The trials would be held at the famous

Red Fort in Delhi, and among the most prominent INA members charged were Colonel Prem Sahgal, Colonel Singh Dhillon, and Major-General Shah Nawaz Khan. These three men had all been high-ranking members of the British Indian Army before they were converted by Bose to serve in the INA.

The fate of these men had more twists and turns than a Hollywood thriller. They had fought for the British, had been taken prisoner by the Japanese, fought with the Japanese, and then taken prisoner by the British. Now, on the eve of what would become India's real push for independence, they were on trial for treason and alleged war crimes.

Yet, due to lack of public support in India and revolts in the British Indian Navy and Army, these efforts were ultimately reversed. Instead of carrying out punishments, the British ended up simply retiring most of the former soldiers from the army and cutting off the pensions of those deemed to be the most troublesome.

India, meanwhile, would indeed be liberated just a couple years after Bose's death, but it wasn't done as the result of a bloody revolution. Instead, it was a matter of arbitrary reform that led to the transfer of power from British to Indian hands. Through the crafting of the Indian Independence Act of 1947, India was divided into the nations we know today as India and Pakistan. The dictates of the act forever partitioned the two regions on religious lines, separating Muslim Pakistan from Hindu India. Mahatma Gandhi hailed the developments as the "noblest act of the British nation."

The partition, however, remains controversial and would kick off a wave of intermittent religious violence for several decades to come, not to mention the fact that Mahatma Gandhi himself would be assassinated by a religious extremist less than a year later. Bose most likely never would have agreed to the partition since he viewed every square inch of historic India as being sacred and indivisible. He also viewed the people as one polity, and those who knew him contend that he would have viewed any separation of Indians—regardless of religious ideation—as complete anathema.

Nevertheless, history marched on without the input of Subhas Chandra Bose, the great Netaji.

Conclusion

The life of Subhas Chandra Bose was in many ways an uncompromising enigma. He was born in the upper echelon of Indian society yet, as a lifelong admirer of both socialism and communism, he sought to tear class structures apart. He despised Indian's old caste system, and in one of his early diatribes, he proclaimed that all Indians should work as one. In his famous words, Bose declared that the "naked Indian, the Brahman Indian, and pariah Indian" all needed to come together to forge one India.

Yet despite these utilitarian claims, he was a young man who very much benefited from his father's affluent position as a prominent lawyer in British India. It was his dad, after all, who famously "threw away 10,000 rupees" so that his son could take examinations to enter into the highly esteemed Indian Civil Services. But even after passing the exams with flying colors, Bose rejected the prestigious position laid at his feet in order to pursue his own revolutionary activities.

Another seeming contradiction was Bose's admiration of Gandhi coupled with his own seemingly unceasing advocacy of violence. Almost anyone would agree that Gandhi and Hitler would make strange bedfellows, yet Subhas Chandra Bose was associated with them both.

But although he may at first glance appear to be a man of contradictions, the one driving focus of his career—indeed of his life—was the independence of India. Perhaps his efforts can be more easily understood in the words of another revolutionary, America's Malcolm X, who declared that change needed to occur by "any means necessary." Because no matter what the situation was, and no matter what people or places Bose made use of, his main overriding goal was to create a free and independent India for the future generations. Some may say that he entered into a Faustian bargain by teaming up with dictators in Germany and Japan, but Bose's desire for a free India was so great that everything else took a backseat. In his eyes, India's plight was of such importance that any of these means he employed justified the ends that he sought.

Whether you view his struggle sympathetically or harshly, one thing is certain—Subhas Chandra Bose was a man of uncommon and uncompromising conviction, the likes of which this world has rarely seen.

Made in the USA
Monee, IL
22 July 2024

62467769R00024